Keeping Pets

STICK INSECTS & MANTIDS

June McNicholas

 Heinemann

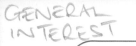

www.heinemann.co.uk/library
Visit our website to find out more information about Heinemann Library books.

To order:
☎ Phone 44 (0) 1865 888066
▤ Send a fax to 44 (0) 1865 314091
▢ Visit the Heinemann Bookshop at www.heinemann.co.uk/library to browse our catalogue and order online.

First published in Great Britain by Heinemann Library, Halley Court, Jordan Hill, Oxford OX2 8EJ
a division of Reed Educational and Professional Publishing Ltd. Heinemann is a registered trademark of Reed Educational and Professional Publishing Ltd.

OXFORD MELBOURNE AUCKLAND JOHANNESBURG BLANTYRE
GABORONE IBADAN PORTSMOUTH (NH) USA CHICAGO

© Reed Educational and Professional Publishing Ltd 2002
First published in paperback 2003
The moral right of the proprietor has been asserted.

Designed by Celia Floyd
Originated by Dot Gradations Limited
Printed by Wing King Tong in Hong Kong/China

ISBN 0 431 12400 0 (hardback)   ISBN 0 431 12403 5 (paperback)
06 05 04 03 02   07 06 05 04 03
10 9 8 7 6 5 4 3 2 1   10 9 8 7 6 5 4 3 2 1

British Library Cataloguing in Publication Data

Stick insects and mantids. – (Keeping unusual pets)
1. Mantidae – Juvenile literature
2. Stick insects as pets – Juvenile literature
638.5'727

Acknowledgements
The Publishers would like to thank the following for permission to reproduce photographs: Ardea London Ltd/Andrea Florence: p.4; Ardea London Ltd/Peter Steyn: pp. 14 (top), 38; Ardea London Ltd/Jim Zipp: p. 8; Bruce Coleman Collection: p. 39 (top); Gareth Boden: pp. 5 (top), 6 (top), 6 (bottom), 7 (top), 7 (bottom), 9 (bottom), 10, 11, 12, 13 (top), 13 (bottom), 16, 17 (top), 17 (bottom), 18, 19, 20, 21, 23 (all pics), 24 (top), 24 (bottom), 25, 26, 27, 28 (top), 29 (bottom), 30, 32, 33 (top), 33 (bottom), 34, 35, 37 (top), 37 (bottom), 39 (bottom), 40, 41, 42, 43 (top), 43 (bottom), 44; NHPA/Stephen Dalton: p. 29 (top); Oxford Scientific Films/Daniel J. Cox: p. 28 (bottom); Oxford Scientific Films/Densey Clyne: p. 14 (bottom); Oxford Scientific Films/Mantis Wildlife Films: p. 31 (top); Oxford Scientific Films/Alistair Shay: p. 9 (top); Science Photo Library: p. 22; Science Photo Library/Dr Morley Read: p. 5 (bottom); Science Photo Library/Ray Coleman: p. 31 (bottom); Science Photo Library/Pascal Goetgheluck: p. 15; Tudor Photography: p. 45 (all pics)

Cover photograph reproduced with permission of Ardea/Andy Teare.

Every effort has been made to contact copyright holders of any material reproduced in this book. Any omissions will be rectified in subsequent printings if notice is given to the Publishers.

Disclaimer
All the Internet addresses (URLs) given in this book were valid at the time of going to press. However, due to the dynamic nature of the Internet, some addresses may have changed, or sites may have changed or ceased to exist since publication. While the author and Publishers regret any inconvenience this may cause readers, no responsibility for any such changes can be accepted by either the author or the Publishers.

No animals were harmed during the process of taking photographs for this series.

Contents

Stick insects and mantids

Keeping stick insects and praying mantids (also called mantises) can be fascinating and fun. These exotic insects range from the beautiful to the peculiar, and give you the chance to appreciate just how interesting insects can be. You may not be able to cuddle insects or take them for walks, but they can still be rewarding pets.

Some stick insects really do look like sticks!

Insect bodies

Insects do not have a bony skeleton inside their body. In fact, they have no bones at all! Instead they have a hard outside casing called an **exoskeleton** ('exo' means outside). This exoskeleton protects their soft body parts. It does not stretch and grow like our skin does, so insects have to shed their skin as they get bigger. This is called **moulting**. It is just like climbing out of a set of clothes that have got too small and leaving them behind!

Three parts

An insect's body is made up of three parts: the head, the **thorax** and the **abdomen**. The head has the mouth parts on its underside, an eye on either side of it and two antennae, or feelers, on top. The antennae allow the insect to feel its way around. They detect changes in the environment, such as the smell of other insects and animals.

4

The thorax is the middle section of an insect's body. All insects have six legs that are attached to the thorax, three on each side. The wings of winged insects are also attached to the thorax.

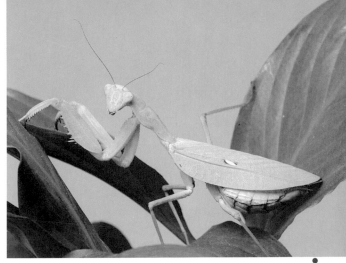

The abdomen contains the insect's **organs** for breathing. Insects do not have lungs like we do. Instead, air is sucked in and out of the abdomen through tiny openings called **spiracles**. In large insects you can sometimes see the abdomen expand and contract as the insect breathes.

All insect bodies have three parts – a head, a thorax and an abdomen. You can see these parts on this mantid.

Did you know?

Although all insects have the same basic body design, different **species**, or types, can look very different from each other.

- Some have very long, thin bodies, while others have short, fat shapes.
- Some have bodies that look like dead leaves or twigs, and others have spines or spikes.

Part of the fascination of keeping insects is the variety of shapes, colours and sizes that you can find.

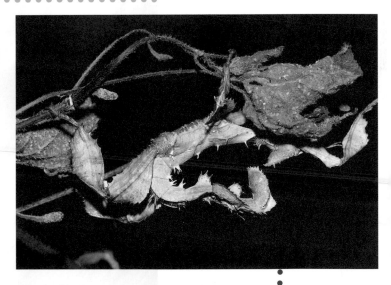

Some insects, like this prickly stick insect from Australia, have spines on their bodies and look like dried-up leaves.

5

Are stick insects and mantids for you?

Stick insects and mantids are a great choice for anyone who is interested in insects and wants to keep unusual pets. They are fairly cheap and easy to care for and do not need as much looking after as cats, dogs or rabbits. They are certainly very interesting, as you can watch them go through their whole **life cycle** – hatching out from eggs, **moulting** and then changing colour, and laying eggs themselves.

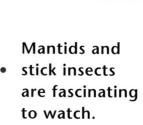

Mantids and stick insects are fascinating to watch.

Good points

- Stick insects and mantids make interesting, unusual pets.
- They are quiet and take up very little space.
- They do not need a lot of time and attention.
- Cleaning is quick and simple.
- Most stick insects and mantids are cheap to buy and to look after.
- You can watch them grow from eggs to adults.

Mantids eat live crickets, but not everyone likes the idea of this!

Not-so-good points

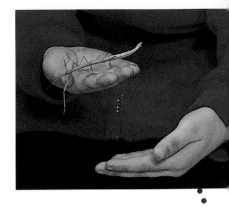

- You need special equipment to keep most stick insects and mantids, and this can be expensive.
- Stick insects and mantids live for only a year or two at the most – not very long compared to most pets.
- They are not cuddly pets. Some stick insects are spiny and painful to touch. Some mantids can bite, although they are not poisonous.
- Mantids need live food such as crickets. These have to be bought and kept until the mantid needs them. Escaped crickets will not be popular with the rest of the family!
- You will need to give your pets fresh food all year round, even in winter.

People can hold some stick insects if they are gentle, but others are too prickly to handle!

Stick insects and mantids are similar sorts of creatures but they have different needs. They have different diets and they also need to be cared for in different ways. This book will look first at stick insects and then at mantids.

Need to know

- It is illegal to bring stick insects or mantids into the country.
- Children are not allowed to buy pets themselves. In any case, you should always have an adult with you when you buy your pet.
- Most countries have laws protecting animals, and this includes insects. Never release stick insects or mantids into the countryside. They will not be able to survive.

Part 1 Stick insects

Stick insect facts

Stick insects belong to a family of insects that scientists call phasmids, which means 'ghosts'. They are called this because they are so difficult to see! There are between 2500 and 3000 known **species** of stick insects and there are probably many more yet to be discovered.

Most stick insects come from very hot countries so they cannot live in the wild in places where the temperature can get very cold. They usually live in trees or shrubs, eating their leaves, but some species live on the ground and feed on plants.

Did you know

Some stick insects have wings. Although they are not good fliers, they can fly for short distances. This means that they can fly to another tree or escape from **predators** such as birds, reptiles or even other insects.

Cunning camouflage

All stick insects are brilliant at **camouflage**, which means they can make themselves almost invisible to avoid being eaten. As their name suggests, many stick insects look just like sticks or small branches. They keep completely still with their legs folded against them to look like a part of the tree. Some even sway a little as if they are blowing in the wind, just like the leaves and twigs around them!

Stick insect bodies can look exactly like a tangle of dry twigs!

8

Many stick insects are the same greens or browns as the plants they live on. Others are even cleverer in their disguise and have bodies that look like leaves or even bird droppings!

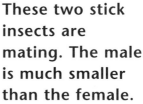

Some species of stick insects look just like the leaves that they feed on.

Male or female?

Male and female stick insects can look quite different, even if they are the same species.

- Often, females are larger than males and sometimes they are a different colour.
- In some species, only one of the sexes (usually the male) has wings.
- Although stick insects are either male or female, some female stick insects do not need to mate with a male to produce eggs!

These two stick insects are mating. The male is much smaller than the female.

Eggs and nymphs

Stick insect eggs can take between three months and a year to hatch – depending on the species. They hatch into tiny, almost see-through, miniature stick insects called **nymphs**. The nymphs grow quickly, **moulting** several times. Some nymphs are fully grown by six months, others take up to eighteen months.

9

Choosing your stick insect

If you are just starting to keep stick insects it is a good idea to contact your local entomological society. **Entomology** is the study of insects, and the members of the society will be able to give you lots of information about different types of stick insects and where you can buy them. You can find out about these societies from your local pet shop, museum or library. Your local pet shop owner may also be able to help you find an insect breeder in your local area.

Insect breeders have a large number of insects for you to choose from. They will also give you advice on how to care for your pets.

How old?

Stick insects can usually be bought as eggs, **nymphs** or adults. There are advantages and disadvantages with all of these. The eggs may not hatch and it is normal for many nymphs to die before they become adults. Stick insects bought as adults have a shorter life span, although they may lay eggs so you can **rear** the next generation. If you are new to stick insects, it is probably best to buy adults as these are easier to keep.

What to look for

- Choose stick insects that look healthy and have no patchy marks on their skin.
- Make sure that they are interested in their food.
- Avoid any insects that do not have all their legs!

What sort?

Stick insects come from a wide range of climates and surroundings. Different **species** eat different plants and need to be kept at different temperatures, so it is very important to know what sort of stick insect you are getting. If you are planning to **breed** stick insects, you must also find out whether you need to keep both sexes.

There are several different species that make good pets. Some of the most common ones are listed over the next few pages, with advice on how to look after them and what to feed them.

Stick insect nymphs are very small and delicate, but if you look after them carefully, some of them will **mature** into adults.

Top tip

Some species of stick insects are not at all easy to keep. They need special heat mats, lamps and **humidity** equipment. So before you buy your stick insects, do some homework! Read about the different varieties and ask advice from insect breeders and societies. There are useful addresses listed at the back of this book.

Indian stick insects

The Indian stick insect is also often known as the laboratory stick insect. It is the most commonly kept stick insect, and is often seen in pet shops and school biology labs. Indian stick insects normally reach a length of about 10 centimetres. They are usually green, greenish yellow or slightly darker if they are about to **moult**.

Indian stick insects are mostly female. Males are slightly smaller and sometimes have a reddish underbelly. Females do not need a male to breed. Adult females lay eggs almost daily.

Indian stick insects have a small red patch at the top of their front legs, which is very visible when they move around.

Indian stick insect care

This species can live quite happily at normal room temperature without extra heating in their tank. If you feel comfortably warm so will your stick insects.

Feeding Indian stick insects is very simple. They eat bramble and privet leaves. One or two **sprays** of leaves in a container of water will provide your insects with fresh food for a few days.

Breeding Indian stick insects

- Indian stick insects drop their eggs onto the ground, so you will need to sort out the eggs from the droppings when you clean out their tank.
- The eggs (right) can take three or four months to hatch.
- Indian stick insect nymphs are fully grown after four to six months and live for up to a year.

Pink-winged stick insects

The pink-winged stick insect comes from Madagascar and East Africa and is also known as the Madagascan stick insect. It has a pale brown body and pale pinky-white wings. Males are slightly smaller than females but most pink-winged stick insects are female. Pink-winged stick insects live for about a year.

Pink-winged stick insects will sometimes try to fly away. If they do, you will need to pick them up very gently.

Pink-winged care

These stick insects do not need a heat mat in their tank, but they do need to be kept in a warm room. An occasional light **misting** of water will help to keep the air in their tank moist.

The favourite food plants of pink-winged stick insects are bramble leaves and rose leaves. Take off any large thorns or prickles that may damage the insects' delicate wings.

Breeding pink-wings

- Female pink-winged stick insects lay eggs without mating.
- They lay their eggs on the underside of the leaves of their food plants, so when you are replacing food make sure you check the leaves before you throw them out.
- The eggs hatch after around two to four months.
- The nymphs will be fully grown and develop their wings at about six to eight months old.

13

Giant prickly stick insects

Giant prickly stick insects, also known as Macleay's Spectre, come from Australia. The females may be up to 20 centimetres long. Both sexes are a brownish colour and have prickly spines on their **abdomen**. The males are usually a little duller in colour than the females and are smaller and less bulky looking. Only male giant pricklies can fly.

Giant prickly care

This species needs special care. The temperature in their tank should be about 25°C and it will need misting daily with warm water to keep the air moist and humid.

Giant pricklies eat bramble leaves, oak leaves, rose leaves and eucalyptus leaves. You will need to pick strong branches to support the weight of these large insects.

Be careful how you handle giant pricklies – they live up to their name and have large prickly bodies!

Breeding giant pricklies

- Giant pricklies need to mate (right) before the female can lay eggs. The eggs are just dropped to the floor.
- If you want to hatch the eggs, you can remove them or place them in a container in the tank.
- The eggs need to be kept at about the same temperature and humidity as the adult insects.
- They may take six months or even a year to hatch!

Jungle nymph stick insects

These large insects come from hot, humid parts of Malaysia. The males are small, brown and have patterned wings. The females are much larger (about 18 centimetres) and are usually bright green, although some may be yellow. The females do not have proper wings, just small wing buds. The bodies of these insects, especially their legs, are covered with sharp spines. This makes handling these insects rather painful if you are not extremely careful!

Jungle nymph care

Jungle nymphs like to eat bramble leaves. The temperature in their tank needs to be kept at a constant 23°C. You will also need to mist the tank daily with warm water, to keep it as humid as the jungles where they come from.

Breeding jungle nymphs

- Female jungle nymphs rarely go down to the ground except to lay their eggs. The female needs a patch of soil to lay her eggs in. A small tub of moist **peat** is ideal.
- Jungle nymph eggs should be kept moist and warm and must not be disturbed. Only a small number will hatch, and this can sometimes take up to 18 months!
- The nymphs grow very slowly and may not mature until they are about 18 months old.
- They may live for another year after becoming fully grown. Jungle nymph stick insects live for a total of about 24–30 months.

Female jungle nymph stick insects are quite large!

Giant spiny stick insects

These large ground-living stick insects come from the island of New Guinea in the Pacific. They are usually a dark, glossy brown and can seem quite creepy because they look rather like scorpions! The females are about 15 centimetres long and their abdomen has a pointed tip. The males measure about 12 centimetres long. They have a blunt end to their abdomen.

Giant spiny stick insects look a bit like scorpions. They have **spurs** on the backs of their legs. Occasionally, if they are alarmed or angry, they can give off a nasty smell – a bit like rotting onions!

Giant spiny care

Giant spinies live mostly on the ground, so they need different housing to the tree-dwelling species. They need a tank with a deep layer of damp peat on the floor and pieces of bark to hide under. They will also need to be able to reach their food plants from the ground. They are fond of bramble and oak leaves.

Giant spinies like to be kept warm, at about 21°C, and need daily misting with warm water. Unlike most other stick insects, they also need water to drink. Remember to change their water daily so that it always remains fresh.

16

Breeding giant spinies

- If you want to breed giant spiny stick insects, you will need to keep both males and females so they can mate.
- Once they have mated, a female will find a patch of damp soil in which to bury her eggs. It is a good idea to put a deep dish in the tank for her to use. The dish should be filled with a mixture of peat and **vermiculite** (a special soil used for pot plants).
- Giant spiny eggs need to be kept moist and warm, like the adult insects. They take between three and six months to hatch, and sometimes even longer.
- The nymphs are very dark brown in colour when they first hatch but then become paler and speckled until they are mature.
- Giant spiny stick insects can live for about two years.

Giant spinies need to drink fresh water. Half fill a shallow lid with water and put it on the floor of their tank.

Giant spinies like to lay their eggs in a mixture of vermiculite and peat.

Handle with care!

You need to be very careful when handling giant spiny stick insects. If they are startled they can drive their leg spurs into your hand hard enough to draw blood! However, most of the time they are peaceful enough. If you have more than one male, you may have to separate them – sometimes they try to fight each other!

What do I need?

The easiest and cheapest way to keep stick insects is in a plastic tank with a lid. Nearly all pet shops stock these.

What size tank?

The size of your tank should depend on how big your stick insects will grow. A good guide is to make sure the height of your tank is double the length of an adult stick insect. Do not keep too many insects in one tank. Half a dozen medium-sized insects in a tank 60 centimetres long, 30 centimetres wide and 45 centimetres high is probably enough.

Your stick insect will need enough room to hang upside down when it moults. This helps it to crawl out of its old skin easily!

Escape alert!

Most plastic tanks have slits in their lids for **ventilation** and tiny **nymphs** can easily escape through these. You will need to reduce the size of the slits by covering both sides with sticky tape. Be very careful not to leave any sticky surfaces that could damage the nymphs' legs.

18

Heat and humidity

If your stick insects need to be kept warmer than normal room temperature, you will need a heat mat. The mat acts like a small electric blanket and can be placed under the tank or against one of its sides. The temperature of the mat is controlled by a **thermostat**. If your tank does not have a thermometer built in, you can use an ordinary room thermometer or a digital aquarium thermometer to check the temperature in your insects' living area.

If you have the kind of stick insect that is used to living in a jungle, you will need a **humidity** meter too. This shows how moist the air is. You can keep the tank humid by **misting** it with a small hand spray filled with warm water, or by placing a shallow dish of water in the tank.

Floor coverings

The type of floor covering needed depends on the sort of stick insect you are keeping.

- Tree-dwelling stick insects live on the branches of their food plant, so just line their tank with paper.
- Stick insects that live on the ground need moist **peat** as a floor covering – a depth of 2 cm is about right. Make sure you remove any mould that develops.
- Insects that lay their eggs on the ground need a small patch of peat and **vermiculite** mixture.

This tank is kept warm by a heat mat. The tank has a thermometer and humidity meter built into its side.

Caring for your stick insect

When you buy your stick insects, make sure that you find out what sort of leaves they feed on! Most stick insects eat bramble leaves but many **species** have a particular favourite, such as privet, rose or oak.

Finding food

Whatever leaves you feed your insects, make sure you know where to get a good supply and find out whether you need permission to pick them. It is best to pick young **sprays** of leaves that are long and strong enough for your insects to clamber about on. Always wash the leaves before feeding them to your insects. They may have been treated with weed killer or **insecticide**. Washing also gets rid of any small insects that could injure your stick insects, especially **nymphs**.

During the winter it may be difficult to find sprays of new leaves. Stick insects will eat older leaves, but cut off any withered brown edges. Alternatively, you could grow your own plants in a pot. Keep your pot indoors in the light, and you will have a ready supply of good quality leaves for your pets.

Place the sprays in a pot of water to keep them fresh. Cover the top of the water pot with paper and then push the sprays through. This will prevent any smaller insects from falling into the water and drowning. Replace the sprays every few days.

Cleaning the tank

Stick insects are not messy animals and their tanks do not need daily cleaning. Replace the floor coverings whenever they look messy or if you notice any mouldy patches of peat. Otherwise, clean out the tank once a week. Empty the tank completely before wiping it down with mild soapy water and drying it thoroughly. It is a good idea to turn the tank upside down to dry for a while. You should also make sure that the tank lid is clean and dry too. The tank must be absolutely dry before you put in clean floor coverings and fresh leaves.

Place your stick insects into a temporary container when cleaning their tank.

Top tip

When you change your pets' food sprays, make sure you remove any tiny nymphs from the branches. Some stick insects lay their eggs on the underside of leaves, so remember to check there too.

Breeding stick insects

Are you planning to **breed** stick insects? The first thing you will need to find out is whether you need to keep males and females. The females of many **species** do not need males to mate. They just lay eggs when they are fully grown.

You will also need to know the egg-laying habits of the species you are keeping – the information on pages 12–17 will help. Do they just drop their eggs on the floor? Do they need a pot of **peat** or **vermiculite** to lay their eggs in? Do they attach their eggs to the underside of leaves? Once you know this, you will know where to look for their eggs!

Collecting eggs

Collect the eggs carefully, separating them from any droppings, which will make them go mouldy. Try to keep the eggs at the same temperature and **humidity** as the adult insects, although you do not need to keep them in the same tank.

Top tip

You may need lots of patience while you wait for the eggs to hatch.

- Some species can hatch in six weeks, but others can take a year or more. Even eggs laid at the same time may not all hatch at once.
- Keeping a note of laying and hatching dates can help, but there may still be a lot of time difference. It is normal for many eggs not to hatch at all.

The eggs of the giant prickly stick insect take up to six months to hatch.

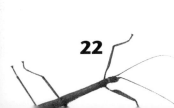

Jungle nymph eggs can take as long as eighteen months to hatch!

Nymphs

Young stick insects are known as **nymphs**. As soon as the nymphs
are hatched, make sure there is food available for them. However, you need to be very careful that the young nymphs do not fall into the water pot and drown. You must also be careful when you are **misting** the tank with water, as some nymphs can drown in even a droplet of water.

Newly hatched nymphs are known as **hatchlings**. They are very tiny and only some of them survive.

Most nymphs will feed well and **moult** frequently until they are about five months old. Most species slow down their growth at this stage, growing much more gradually until they are ready to **breed**.

Nymphs are very delicate and you should not handle them. If you need to move them, try to do so only by picking up the leaf they are on, or by getting them to hold on to a small brush – such as a make-up brush.

23

Part 2 Mantids

What is a mantid?

In some ways, mantids (also called mantises) are very similar to stick insects. They usually live in hot countries, and perch in trees, where they are cleverly **camouflaged**. They have similar bodies to stick insects and live for about the same amount of time – one to two years. However, mantids have huge eyes and a head that is able to turn from side to side. When you look at a mantid, it turns and looks back at you!

Another difference between stick insects and mantids is their legs. Mantids' front legs are long and drawn up under their head, as if they are praying. This is how they get the name 'praying mantis'.

There is something about a mantid that makes it look as if it knows what you are thinking!

Mantids spend a lot of time on four legs with their upper body and forelegs raised up, as if they were praying.

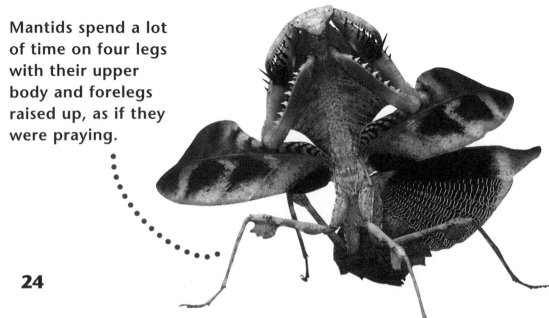

Mantids are hunters

Perhaps the biggest single difference between stick insects and mantids is the food that they eat. Mantids are **carnivorous**. This means that they eat living creatures – not plants. Their diet is mostly other insects, although they will also eat small **grubs** or caterpillars from time to time.

Mantids sit and wait for their **prey**, watching for the slightest movement that could mean food. They are so well camouflaged that the insect does not know they are there. When the mantid sees a suitable target, it shoots out its front legs and grabs the insect. The jagged edges on the mantid's legs stop the insect from escaping. The mantid then brings the insect up to its mouth and eats it – while it is still alive!

The mantid grasps its prey firmly in its jagged front legs and then swallows it.

Choosing your mantid

Many large pet shops stock the common types of mantid, and some reptile magazines contain advertisements for **exotic** insect suppliers. However, it is best to contact your local **entomological** society. They will be able to recommend the best places to buy mantids. That way you can make sure that your insects have been well looked after and have been **bred** in **captivity** and not captured from the wild.

Insect breeders sell a wide range of mantids, and also stock supplies of their food.

What sort?

Like stick insects, mantids come in many shapes and colours. Some are very beautiful, and others just look really weird. It is important to know what **species** of mantid you are buying, and how it needs to be cared for in order to stay healthy. However, all mantids need to be kept in a warm and **humid** environment.

Breeding

- If you want to breed mantids, you must have a male and female. Unlike many stick insects, mantids need to mate before the female can lay eggs.
- The male and female both need to be fully grown in order to mate successfully, but males and females may **mature** at different ages. If you buy **nymphs** of the same age, the male may become too old to mate before the female is ready! For more information about breeding mantids, see pages 38–39.

Not too fancy!

Do not be tempted by very unusual species of mantids. Some types need specialist care and will almost certainly die unless you are very experienced in keeping exotic insects. Get used to keeping the more common varieties first – you will actually find it more enjoyable. Some suitable species for beginners are described on the next few pages.

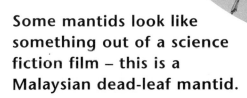

Some mantids look like something out of a science fiction film – this is a Malaysian dead-leaf mantid.

Common mantids

The four mantids shown on these two pages are often kept as pets. They will be happy in a plastic tank with a floor covering of pebbles, sand or wood chippings. The tank will need to be kept at a temperature of around 23°C and the humidity level should be between 50 per cent and 60 per cent.

African mantis

This is probably the most commonly kept mantid. It is usually an attractive bright green colour. Both males and females have wings and can fly. The female grows to about eight centimetres long. She is slightly bigger and heftier looking than the male of the species.

The African mantis is probably the best species for first-time mantid owners. It is straightforward to keep, and has very few problems with **moulting** or breeding.

The African mantis is a very attractive insect. It is also one of the easiest mantids to look after.

Common European mantis

The common European mantis has a slim body which is usually pale green or beige. It measures about seven centimetres long and comes from the Mediterranean area. Like the African mantis, it is easy to keep.

The common European mantis is a good choice for an inexperienced mantis keeper.

Madagascan mantis

This species is found on the island of Madagascar and in some parts of East Africa. Madagascan mantids frequently live in houses, where people find them valuable as fly catchers! The Madagascan mantis is quite large – it measures about nine centimetres long – and is an enthusiastic hunter. If it mistakes your finger for an insect it will bite it hard!

The Madagascan mantis can be quite fierce, so it needs careful handling.

Egyptian mantis

The Egyptian mantis is a small and slender insect which rarely grows more than four centimetres long. It is a pretty creature, usually pale greenish-yellow or light brownish-yellow in colour.

Although it looks delicate, the Egyptian mantis makes quite a good pet for a beginner.

Exotic mantids

Exotic mantids can be extremely beautiful, but these species are usually much more expensive than the common varieties. Sometimes they are also quite difficult to look after, so it is a good idea to get lots of experience before you buy one.

Dead-leaf mantids

There are a number of mantids with bodies that look like dead leaves. A dead-leaf mantid will nestle in real leaves, hiding from a **predator**. If it feels really threatened it will drop out of the tree to the ground – just like a dead leaf!

Dead-leaf mantids need warm temperatures of 25–27°C and about 80 per cent humidity. A floor covering of **peat** or **vermiculite** will help to keep their tank moist.

Exotic care

Exotic mantids need very special care. Here are a few of the things you will need to think about.

- Exotic mantids often need high temperatures and high humidity levels.
- Shedding old skin off such odd-shaped bodies can lead to **deformities**.
- Mantids that look like flowers usually feed on insects that drink the **nectar** of flowers. This means they need a richer diet than ordinary mantids.

Dead-leaf mantids look like scruffy, dried up leaves.

Flower mantids

Most flower mantids come from Africa, Asia and South America. As the name suggests, they have bodies that **mimic** flowers. This helps the mantids to catch small insects which mistake them for flowers and settle within easy catching distance.

Because most flower mantids are from **tropical** areas, they need temperatures of around 24°C and humidity levels of around 70 per cent. You should always remember to ask your supplier about the needs of the particular species that you are buying.

This Borneo flower mantid has legs shaped like petals to help it **camouflage** itself.

Orchid mantids

Orchid mantids are the most spectacular of the flower-mimicking mantids. They need higher temperatures (25–27°C), greater humidity and often a specialist diet. They are definitely not the right mantid for a beginner!

Orchid mantids are very beautiful, but they are expensive to buy and hard work to look after.

What do I need?

You will need a basic tank for your mantid. This can be the same kind of plastic tank that stick insects are kept in. A tank measuring about 30 centimetres high, 30 centimetres long and 20 centimetres wide will be big enough for most adult mantids, but make sure your mantid has plenty of room to hang upside down from the lid when it **moults**. Buy a tank with a secure plastic lid with small **ventilation** slits in it.

You will need to place a heat mat under your tank to keep it warm. Many tanks are fitted with a thermometer and a humidity meter so you can check that the air inside the tank is warm and moist.

Essential equipment

Mantids need a warm, moist environment so you will need to buy a heat mat to heat the tank, and a water bottle so you can **mist** the sides of the tank regularly. You will also need a thermometer to check the temperature inside the tank and a **humidity** meter to check how moist the air is. These are very important because most mantids will soon become ill if the temperature and humidity in their tank are not right.

Furnishing the tank

Try to make the tank look and feel like your mantid's natural surroundings. For mantids that live in the desert, add sand, gravel and pebbles, with perhaps a few pieces of dry bark and shrubby branches. For jungle mantids, you can grow real plants and flowers for them to climb about on, and use silk or plastic ones, too. Paper flowers are not a good idea in a humid tank – they will end up as messy pulp!

Desert mantids will like sand or gravel on the bottom of their tank and some bark and pebbles to climb around on.

If you keep a jungle mantid, you can make its tank look really striking.

One or more?

Most mantids are cannibals, which means they eat other mantids. Because of this, it is best to play safe and keep only one in a tank!

Caring for your mantid

Mantids eat live insects, so you will need a ready supply of food. Most mantid keepers feed crickets to their mantids. You can buy crickets from a pet shop. They come in different sizes, from tiny **hatchlings** to fully-grown adults, but adult crickets are not suitable for mantids.

Cricket care

Crickets are usually bought from a pet shop in a small cardboard box like an egg box. This can be kept in a plastic container with a secure lid, or the crickets can be placed in a small tank of their own. Most insect keepers add a few twigs or pieces of bark for them to shelter under. They will also need feeding. A piece of fruit such as a ripe apple will keep them happy, but replace it when it starts to shrivel.

Keep it small!

It is important that you feed the right sized food to your mantid. Crickets do not want to be eaten so they will fight back. A cricket that is too large for the mantid may damage it with its strong legs. Keep on the safe side and feed only small insects to your mantids.

You can buy cricket hatchlings in containers from pet shops. Keep the container in a cool place.

How often?

Most adult mantids only need feeding once or twice a week. Just pop a cricket or two into the tank and wait for your mantid to snatch them. Remove any bits and pieces the mantid does not eat. Also remove any live insects that are not eaten – they may attack your mantid later. This can be especially dangerous if your mantid is still soft-skinned after recently **moulting**.

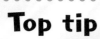

Top tip

Put your crickets in a bag in the fridge for an hour before you give them to your mantid. This will make them more sluggish and less likely to put up a fight!

Special diets

Some mantids need a special diet. Flower mantids often eat insects that feed on **nectar** from flowers. These insects are a richer form of food than crickets. You cannot usually buy these small nectar insects (although a few insect breeders supply them) so you will have to feed your flower mantids other rich food. Some of these mantids eat wax-worms, but you should ask your breeder or supplier what they recommend.

Mantids eat live crickets! Make sure the crickets are not too big or they might start attacking your pet!

Keep it clean

Mantids are very clean animals. They spend a large part of their time grooming and cleaning themselves. As they produce very little waste their tanks do not need cleaning out very often. The most important thing is to remove bits of uneaten food. This usually means pieces of cricket! These will go mouldy and cause health problems for your pet if they are left in the tank.

Most cleaning will be just a quick picking out of leftover food and dead leaves, but you will need to give the tank a thorough clean every week or two.

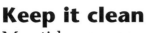

Top tips

- Keep an eye on any flowers and plants in your mantid's tank. These can get **mildewed** and be unhealthy for your mantid.
- If your mantid has some bark in its tank, check that it is not mouldy on the underneath.

Cleaning your tank

First place your mantid in a safe temporary container, so it does not escape or get harmed by any of the cleaning materials you are using. Then empty out the tank and wipe around it with warm soapy water. Do not use strong detergents, bleach or anything with **insecticides** in it! Rinse and dry everything thoroughly before you replace the contents.

Holiday care

If you are away for more than a few days, you should ask a reliable friend or neighbour to look after your mantid. They will need to check the temperature and **humidity** in its tank, clear away any mess and make sure that it has fresh food and water. Remember to explain everything that needs to be done before you leave – it may help to compile a checklist.

Keep your mantid safely in a container while you are cleaning out its tank.

Taking care

Some of the greatest dangers to your pets happen by accident.

- Do not let your mantids get too cold. If the heating in the tank fails, or the room gets too cold, they will quickly die.
- Make sure your mantids are not too hot – keep their tank away from direct sunlight and be careful not to turn up the thermostat on your heat pad too much.
- Do not spray your room with fly-killer or insecticide.
- Do not use flea-spray on your cat or dog if it is likely to be in the same room as your insects.
- Avoid using disinfectant sprays or paint stripper near your mantid's tank.

You must keep a close eye on your tank's humidity meter and thermometer . Mantids can die very quickly if they get too hot or too cold.

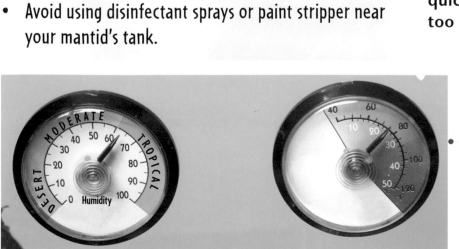

Breeding mantids

If you plan to **breed** mantids, you will need to buy a male and a female of the same **species**. This is not always easy because both sexes need to be fully adult before they can breed, but males and females often **mature** at different rates. If you buy **nymphs** of the same age the male may be too old to mate by the time the female becomes **fertile**, so you may need to buy in an older male.

Laying eggs

About one month after she has mated, the female will produce a foamy looking mass, usually at the top of her tank or on a branch. This is an egg container called an **ootheca**. The container soon hardens to protect the hundreds of eggs inside. A female may produce one or several oothecas after mating.

Fact or fiction?

It is a common belief that female mantids eat the male while they are mating. This is not always true, although a hungry female will not think twice about eating a mate! It has also been known for the male to mistake his future mate for his next meal! It is therefore best to introduce a male and a female when they have both recently had a good meal. You should remove the male after they have mated.

A female mantid will stay close to her ootheca after producing it, making sure that her eggs are safe.

Hatching

After three to four weeks, the ootheca breaks open and tiny **hatchling** mantids fall to the ground on fine silky strands. After the hatchlings have emerged, the mother should be removed. They do not need her and she might mistake them for food!

Feeding nymphs

Most mantid hatchlings eat tiny flies. Some pet shops stock extremely small fruit flies that are suitable. Almost certainly, some of the nymphs will eat each other. However, it is possible for a good number of nymphs to reach maturity.

This highly magnified photograph shows a hatchling eating a fruit fly.

Sometimes hundreds of nymphs hatch from one ootheca, but only a few of them survive.

Part 3 Caring for your pets

Handling stick insects and mantids

Stick insects and mantids are not cuddly creatures, but there will be times when you want to handle them, or need to move them from one tank to another. You need to be careful not to damage their delicate bodies and wings while you are handling them. Fragile legs can easily break and feet can get torn off if they get caught up in your clothes.

Handle with care

The best way to handle a stick insect or a mantid is to encourage it to walk onto a branch or stick that you are holding. That way you will not damage it by trying to pick it up. From there you can get it to walk onto your hand. If you do have to pick up your pet, gently grasp the insect's body behind its front legs and lift it slowly, taking care not to jerk its legs and feet. The sticky feet will feel like velcro on your skin but they can get badly stuck on clothes or other material.

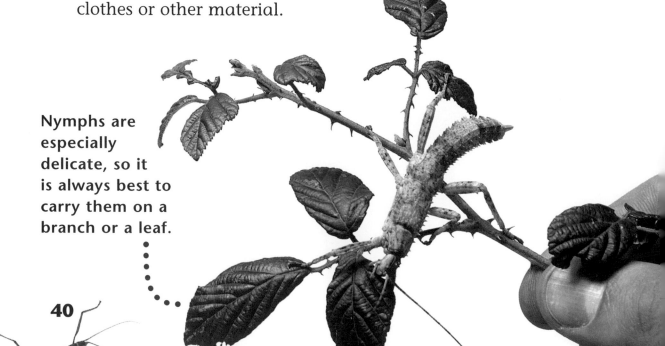

Nymphs are especially delicate, so it is always best to carry them on a branch or a leaf.

40

Top tip

Stick insects with wings need extra care when you are handling them. Besides having very delicate wings, they could fly off! Keep an eye on the wings for any movement that may suggest they are about to take off. Experienced insect keepers say that they can tell when this is going to happen because the middle legs start to twitch before the wings open.

Hands off!

Very young mantids and stick insects should not be handled. They are too delicate for even the gentlest of hands. Move the leaf or plant that they are sitting on instead. Stick insects and mantids that have just **moulted** are also very fragile and should not be handled for a few days after shedding their skin.

Spines and spurs

Although you need to be careful not to hurt your stick insect or mantid when you handle it, you may also have to be careful that it does not hurt you! Some stick insects have sharp spines on their bodies or **spurs** on their legs which they can attack you with. The male giant spiny stick insect can make your fingers bleed! It is often better to hold these insects on a twig.

Sometimes you will need to rescue an insect that has flown off. Encourage it to walk onto your hand and then hold it very gently.

Some health problems

Stick insects and mantids are usually healthy, but they may suffer from a few health problems.

Moulting problems

When a stick insect or a mantid sheds its skin, it should just be able to wriggle out of its old skin and come out with a new one. However, it is not unusual for this to go badly wrong. Occasionally an insect will not **moult** completely, and may leave a leg behind. While stick insects can usually manage with fewer than normal legs, it can be a problem for stick insects that need to climb. Mantids need both their front legs to catch their **prey**, so losing a leg is even more of a problem for them than it is for stick insects.

Sometimes stick insects and mantids lose one of their legs when they moult.

Top tip

When misting the tank, let a few drops of water form on a leaf or two. Many mantids like to drink from these.

Why does it happen?

Sometimes, insects have problems moulting because the air in their tank is too dry. You can increase the moisture in the tank by **misting** more often. However, you should be careful not to overdo it. Too much moisture can make mould grow inside the tank or a fungus grow on your insects.

This mantid has lost parts of its body during its moult.

This mantid has moulted properly. Its body is undamaged and its new skin looks healthy.

Eating problems

If your pet is not due to moult and is not eating there may be something wrong with the food you are offering, or your pet may be too cold.

- Try increasing the warmth in the tank a little.
- For stick insects, try offering fresh food leaves, or even a change of food.
- For mantids, some extra warmth and **humidity** and a fresh cricket often does the trick.
- It is normal for stick insects and mantids to stop eating just before they moult. This is nothing to worry about.

Keeping a record

Keeping records is an important part of being an insect keeper. Some people think it is best to have one record book for each **species** so you can compare individuals of the same species. Other people prefer to record each insect in its own 'file' and then store the records in a loose-leaf folder.

Starting your record

When you first get your insects, note down what species they are, and what date you bought them. Keep a note of what temperature their tank should be kept at, what levels of **humidity** they need and what sort of food they like. You can also write down how often your insects should **moult**, and how long their eggs will take to hatch. This will be very helpful if you forget any of the instructions you have been given.

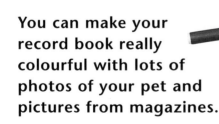

You can make your record book really colourful with lots of photos of your pet and pictures from magazines.

Important information

There are many stages in your insect's life that you can record. Eventually, you will be able to build up a complete picture of its **life cycle**.

- When did your insect moult?
- When did it mate?
- When did it lay its eggs?
- When did the eggs hatch?
- How were the eggs kept until they hatched?
- How many nymphs survived from each hatch?

Ask a friend or relative to take pictures of you and your insect together.

A special diary

As well as including important records, you can write down some of the weird and wonderful things your insects do. Take lots of photos to stick in your record book. They will remind you of all the different stages in each insect's life!

Just the beginning?

Many people start to keep common stick insects and mantids when they are children and then go on to keep different types of insects throughout their lives. Some insect keepers even become famous scientists and have new species named after them! Perhaps buying your first insects will be the start of a lifetime of studying stick insects or mantids!

Your record book will remind you of all the fun you had with your pets.

Why not share your hobby with friends? Maybe then they will want to keep stick insects or mantids too!

45

Glossary

abdomen end section of an insect's body

antennae feelers on an insect's head

breed produce offspring

camouflage to blend in with the surroundings

captivity under the control of humans

carnivorous mainly meat-eating

deformity strange body shape caused by a problem in moulting or growing

entomology the study of insects

exoskeleton skeleton, shell or case on the outside of an animal's body

exotic unusual

fertile able to produce offspring

groom to clean a creature's body; creatures often groom themselves

grub small caterpillar or maggot

hatchlings very young insects that have only just hatched from their eggs

humidity moisture in the air

insecticide chemical that kills insects

life cycle all of a creature's life from birth to death

mature to become adult or fully-grown

mildewed mouldy

mimic to pretend to be something else

mist spray lightly with water

moult to shed an old skin and reveal a new one

nectar sugary liquid found in flowers

nymph young insect, not yet fully grown

ootheca egg case of a mantid

organ part of the body that has a specifc purpose

peat type of soil

predator hunter

prey creature that is hunted for food

rear to look after a creature from when it is young until it is fully grown

species a kind or particular sort of plant or animal

spiracle small air vent on an insect's body

spray small branch of leaves

spur spike on the leg of an insect

thermostat device that controls the temperature of something, for example an insect tank

thorax middle section of an insect's body

tropical hot and humid

ventilation letting in of air

vermiculite special soil used for pot plants

Useful addresses

There are several national societies for people who are interested in keeping and studying insects.

UK

The Phasmid Study Group,
'Papillon',
40 Thorndike Road,
Slough, Berkshire,
SL2 1SR.

The Amateur Entomologists' Society,
PO Box 8774,
London,
SW7 5ZG

AUSTRALIA

The Australian Insect Farm
P.O. Box 26
Innisfail
Queensland 4860

Insektus (Insect education and fun)
P.O. Box 138
Macarthur Square
NSW 2560

To find an **entomological** society anywhere else in the world, go to www.sciref.org/links/EntSoc/index.htm

More books to read

Here are a few basic books that give helpful advice on keeping stick insects or mantids:

Keeping stick insects, Dorothy Floyd (Floyd Publishing, 1987)
Your first praying mantis, Russell Willis (Kingdom Books, 1999)
Your first stick insect, David Alderton (Kingdom Books, 1998)

Helpful websites

www.petbugs.com – Useful website containing lots of useful information on how to care for your pets.
www.insectfarm.com.au – The website of the Australian Insect Farm (see above)
www.wildscenes.com.au/insektus – The website of Insektus (see above)
www.stickinsect.org.uk – The website of the Phasmid Study Group (see above)
www.theaes.org – The website of the Amateur Entomologists' Society (see above)

Index